초등 **영어문장규칙** 배우기

기초문장·단어 따라쓰기

2

와이 앤 엠

차 례

1. 문장의 구조--4

  (a) We are~ · They are~ 4

  · 가족 · 친구---10

  (b) I play ~ We like~ --- 14

  · 운동. 취미 --- 20

  (c) I have~ --- 24

  · 옷 · 악세서리 --- 30

  (d) Let's~ --- 34

  · 삶 --- 40

2. 부정문 만드는 법--44

  (a) I am not He is not--44

  · 대립어1------50

  (b) They are not-- 54

  · 부사,전치사-----60

  (c) I am not, No, I'm not--64

  · 동사 2---70

3. 의문문 만드는 법--74

  (a) Are you~ -- 74

  · 삶.직업-------80

  (b) Are you~--84

  · 우주.자연-----90

  (c) I don't like--94

  · 음식과 과일------100

  (d) Is it~-- 104

  · 대립어 2-----110

  · 직업 2-----114

  · 발음기호 2-----116

초등 영어문장규칙 배우기

기초문장·단어 따라쓰기

2

1. 문장의 구조

(a) We are~ · They are~

We are family.
[wi ər fæməli]

우리는 가족이다

We are classmates.
[wi ər klæsmeit]

우리는 같은 반 친구이다

They are friends.
[ðei ər frendz]

그들은 친구이다

We are family.   We are family.

We are family.   We are family.

We are classmates. We are classmates.

We are classmates. We are classmates.

They are friends. They are friends.

They are friends. They are friends.

They are men.
[ðei ər mæn]

그들은 남자입니다

We are ladies.
[wi ər lé idiz]

우리는 숙녀입니다

They are brothers.
[ðei ər brʌðər]

그들은 형제입니다

문장을 따라 써 보세요

They are men.　They are men.

They are men.　They are men.

We are ladies.　We are ladies.

We are ladies.　We are ladies.

They are brothers.　They are brothers.

They are brothers.　They are brothers.

주어가 단수일 때와 복수일 때, be동사는 어떻게 바뀌나 함께 봅시다.

주어가 하나 (한 명)를 가리킬 때	나	너	그	그녀	그것
	I	You	He	She	It
주어가 둘(두 명) 이상을 가리킬 때	우리	너희	그(녀)들, 그것들		
	We	You	They		

보기에서 골라 〖　　　　〗 속에 알맞은 단어를 쓰고 아래 따라 써 봅시다.

❶ 〖　　　　〗 ladies.

우리는 숙녀이다

ladies.

❷ 〖　　　　〗 friends.

그들은 친구이다

friends.

❸ 〖　　　　〗 brothers.

그들은 형제이다

brothers.

4   classmates.

우리는 같은 반 친구이다

classmates.

5   men.

그들은 남자이다

men.

6   family.

우리는 가족이다

family.

가족 · 친구

mom
엄마

[mam 맘]

mom mom mom mom

uncle
아저씨

[ʌ́ŋkl 엉끌]

uncle   uncle   uncle   uncle

parent
부모님

[pέərənt
페어런트]

parent parent parent parent

sister
여자형제, 언니

[sistər 씨스털]

sister   sister   sister

son
아들

[sɔn 썬]

son   son   son   son   son

relatives 친척 [rélətivz 릴레티브]	relatives　relatives　relatives
daughter 딸 [dɔ́:tər 더-러]	daughter　daughter　daughter
family 가족 [fǽməli 페믈리]	family　family　family
brother 형제 [brʌ́ðr 브롸덜]	brother　brother　brother　brother
cousin 사촌, 친척 [kʌ́zn 커즌]	cousin　cousin　cousin　cousin
ma'am 아주머니, 선생님(여교사) [mæm 맘]	ma'am　ma'am　ma'am　ma'am

life
생명, 생활

[lɑif 라이프]

life life life life life life

live
살다

[liv 리브]

live live live live live

people
사람들, 국민

[píːpl 피-쁠]

people people people people

classmate
동급생

[klǽsméit 클래스메이트]

classmate classmate

grade
학년

[greid 그레드]

grade grade grade grade

library
도서관

[láibreri 라이브러리]

library library library

address
주소

[ædres 어드레스]

address   address   address

stamp
우표

[stæmp스탬프]

stamp   stamp   stamp

letter
편지

[létər 레러]

letter   letter   letter   letter

club
클럽, 동호회

[klʌb 클럽]

club   club   club   club

team
팀

[tiːm 팀]

team   team   team   team

group
무리, 모임, 떼

[gruːp 그루웁]

group   group   group   group

I play soccer.
[ái plei sákər]

나는 축구를 합니다

We like music.
[wi laik mjuːzik]

우리는 음악을 좋아합니다

We like to eat.
[wi laik tuː iːt]

우리는 먹는 것을 좋아합니다

문장을 따라 써 보세요

I play soccer.　　I play soccer.

I play soccer.　　I play soccer.

We like music.　　We like music.

We like music.　　We like music.

We like to eat.　　We like to eat.

We like to eat.　　We like to eat.

I play baseball.
[ái plei beisbɔːl]

나는 야구를 합니다

We study Chinese.
[wi stʌdi tʃɑrniːz]

우리는 중국어를 공부합니다

I like music.
[ái laik mjuːzik]

나는 음악을 좋아합니다

I play baseball. I play baseball.

I play baseball. I play baseball.

We study Chinese. We study Chinese.

We study Chinese. We study Chinese.

I like music.   I like music.

I like music.   I like music.

• play 는 '~를 하다'할 때 씁니다. 예-'~play soccer(~축구를 한다)'. like는 '~을 좋아하다'라고 할 때 씁니다. 예-'~like sports. 스포츠를 좋아한다.'

보기에서 골라 ▢ 속에 알맞은 단어를 쓰고 아래 따라 써 봅시다.

보기   play   like   study

❶ We ▢ music.

우리는 음악을 좋아한다

We _____ music.

❷ I ▢ baseball.

나는 야구를 한다

I _____ baseball.

❸ We ▢ Chinese.

우리는 중국어를 공부한다

你很漂亮

We _____ Chinese.

❹ I 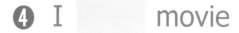 movie

나는 영화를 좋아한다

I　　　　　　movie.

❺ We 　　　 soccer.

우리는 축구를 한다

We　　　　soccer.

❻ We 　　　 tennis.

우리는 테니스를 한다

We　　　　tennis.

❼ I 　　　 sport.

나는 운동을 좋아한다

I　　　　　sport.

단어를 따라 써 보세요

art
미술, 예술

[ɑːrt 알트]

art　art　art　art　art　art

baseball
야구

[béisbɔ̀ːl베이스볼]

baseball　baseball

basketball
농구

[béisbɔ́ːl배스킷볼]

basketball basketball basketball

camera
카메라

[kǽmərə
캐므러]

camera　camera　camera

club
클럽, 동호회

[klʌb 클럽]

club　club　club　club　club

exercise
운동, 연습

[éksərsáiz 액썰싸이즈]

exercise exercise exercise

dance
춤, 춤추다

[dæns 댄스]

dance dance dance

drum
북, 드럼

[drʌm 드럼]

drum drum drum drum

film
필름, 영화

[film 필름]

film film film film film film

football
미식축구

[fútbɔ́ːl 풋볼]

football football football

game
게임

[geim 게임]

game game game game

marathon
마라톤

[mǽrəθən 매러썬]

marathon marathon marathon

movie
영화

[múːvi 무-뷔]

movie   movie   movie   movie

music
음악

[mjúːzik 뮤-직]

music   music   music

photograph
사진

[fóutəgrǽf
포터그래프]

photograph   photograph

rafting
래프팅

[rǽftiŋ 래프팅]

rafting   rafting   rafting   rafting

skating
스케이팅

[skéitiŋ
스케이팅]

skating   skating   skating

soccer
축구

[sákər 싸컬]

soccer soccer soccer

sport
스포츠

[spɔːrt스포-올트]

sport   sport   sport   sport

team
팀

[tiːm 팀]

team team team team team

tennis
테니스

[ténis 테니스]

tennis tennis tennis

travel
여행

[trǽvəl트래블]

travel   travel   travel   travel

volleyball
배구

[valibɔ́ːl발리블]

volleyball volleyball volleyball

(c) I have~

We have one hobby.
[wi hæv wʌn hɑːbi]

우리는 각각 취미를 가지고 있다

We have many books.
[wi hæv meni buks]

우리는 많은 책을 가지고 있다

They have blue jeans.
[ðei hæv bluː dʒiːnz]

그들은 청바지를 가지고 있다

문장을 따라 써 보세요

We have one hobby. We have one hobby.

We have one hobby. We have one hobby.

We have many books. We have many books.

We have many books. We have many books.

They have blue jeans. They have blue jeans.

They have blue jeans. They have blue jeans.

You have a red T-shirt.
[jə hæv ɔː red t-ʃɜːrt]

너는 붉은 티셔츠를 가지고 있다

You have many stamps.
[jə hæv meni stæmps]

너는 많은 우표를 가지고 있다

I have many friends.
[ái hæv meni frenz]

나는 친구가 많다

You have a red T-shirt. You have a red T-shirt.

You have a red T-shirt. You have a red T-shirt.

You have many stamps. You have many stamps.

You have many stamps. You have many stamps.

I have many friends. I have many friends.

I have many friends. I have many friends.

주어가 1,2인칭 복수일 때는 have	주어가 3인칭 단수일 때는 has
I have	She has
You have	He has
We have	It has
They have	Min su has

 보기에서 골라 ░░░░░░░ 속에 알맞은 단어를 쓰고 아래 따라 써 봅시다.

보기	have	has

❶ I ░░░░ many friends.

나는 친구가 많다

I _____ many friends.

❷ They ░░░░ blue jeans.

그들은 청바지를 가지고 있다.

They _____ blue jeans.

❸ We ░░░░ one hobby.

우리는 각각 취미를 가지고 있다

We _____ one hobby.

❹ Do you ⬚⬚⬚ a red pen?

너는 붉은 펜을 가지고 있니?

Do you ⬚⬚⬚ a red pen?

❺ Yes, I ⬚⬚⬚ one.

응, 붉은 펜 하나 가지고 있어.

Yes, I ⬚⬚⬚ one.

❻ Do you ⬚⬚⬚ a books?

너는 책을 가지고 있니?

Do you ⬚⬚⬚ a books?

❼ Do you ⬚⬚⬚ a pink T-shirt?

너는 핑크색 스웨터를 가지고 있니?

Do you ⬚⬚⬚ a pink T-shirt?

단어를 따라 써 보세요

boots
부츠

[buːts 부-츠]

boots   boots   boots   boots

blouse
블라우스

[bláus 블라우스]

blouse   blouse   blouse

button
단추, 버튼

[bΛtn 버튼]

button button button button

cap
모자

[kæp 캡]

cap cap cap cap cap cap

clothes
옷

[klouðz클로우쓰]

clothes clothes clothes

30

coat
외투
[kout 코웃]

coat coat coat coat

dress
의복
[dres 드뢰스]

dress dress dress

glove
장갑
[glʌv 글러브]

glove glove glove glove

hat
모자
[hæt 햇]

hat hat hat hat

jacket
재킷
[dʒǽkit 줴킷]

jacket jacket jacket jacket

pants
바지
[pænts 팬츠]

pants pants pants pants

ribbon
리본

[ríbə 뤼번]

ribbon ribbon ribbon

ring
반지

[riŋ 륑]

ring ring ring ring

sandals
샌들

[sǽndlz샌들즈]

sandals sandals sandals

scarf
목도리

[skáːrt스카-프]

scarf scarf scarf scarf

shirt
셔츠

[ʃəːrt 셜트]

shirt shirt shirt shirt

shoe
신, 구두

[ʃuː 슈-]

shoe shoe shoe shoe

shorts
반바지

[ʃɔ́ːrtʃ 쇼-츠]

shorts   shorts   shorts   shorts

skirt
스커트

[skəːrt 치마]

skirt   skirt   skirt   skirt

sock
양말

[sak 싹]

sock   sock   sock   sock

suit
정장

[súːt 수-트]

suit   suit   suit   suit

sweater
스웨터

[swétər 스웨터]

sweater   sweater

swimsuit
수영복

[swímsùːt
스임수-트]

swimsuit   swimsuit   swimsuit

(d) Let's~

Let's go camping.
[letz gou kæmpiŋ]

캠핑 가자!

Let's go out to play.
[letz gou aut tuː plei]

나가 놀자!

Let's go out here.
[letz gou aut hir]

여기서 나가자!

Let's go camping.   Let's go camping.

Let's go camping.   Let's go camping.

Let's go out to play.   Let's go out to play.

Let's go out to play.   Let's go out to play.

Let's go out to here.   Let's go out to here.

Let's go out to here.   Let's go out to here.

Let's play baseball.
[letz plei beisbɔ:l]

야구하자!

Let's play soccer.
[letz plei sákər]

축구하자!

Let's study.
[letz stʌdi]

공부하자!

문장을 따라 써 보세요

Let's play baseball. Let's play baseball.

Let's play baseball. Let's play baseball.

Let's play soccer.   Let's play soccer.

Let's play soccer.   Let's play soccer.

Let's study.   Let's study.

Let's study.   Let's study.

• Let's는 Let us의 단축형으로 '~하자'의 뜻이며, 무엇인가를 함께 하기를 권유할 때 사용합니다.

🐞 보기에서 골라 ▨▨▨▨ 속에 알맞은 단어를 쓰고 아래 따라 써 봅시다.

❶ _____ out here.

여기서 나가자!

_____

out here.

❷ _____ out to play.

나가 놀자!

_____

out to play.

❸ _____ camping.

캠핑가자!

_____

camping.

4 study.

공부하자!

study.

5 play soccer.

축구하자!

play soccer.

6 play baseball.

야구하자!

play baseball.

7 eat pizza!

피자 먹자!

eat pizza!

단어를 따라 써 보세요

east
동쪽

[iːst 이스트]

east east east east

idea
생각

[aidːə 아이디어]

idea idea idea idea

life
생명, 생활

[laif 라이프]

life life life life life life

live
살다

[liv 리브]

live live live live live live

luck
행운

[lɔk 럭]

luck luck luck luck luck luck

map
지도

[mæp 맵]

map map map map

matter
문제, 곤란

[mǽter 매터]

matter matter matter matter

news
소식

[njuːz 뉴-즈]

news news news news

north
북쪽

[nɔːrθ 놀쓰]

north north north north

party
파티, 모임

[páːrti 파-티]

party party party party party

pay
지불하다

[pei 페이]

pay pay pay pay pay

peace
평화
[piːs 피-스]

peace   peace   peace   peace

people
사람들, 국민
[piːpl 피-쁠]

people people people

place
장소, 곳
[pleis 플레이스]

place place place place place

road
길, 도로
[roud 로우드]

road   road   road

sleep
잠자다
[sliːp 슬리-입]

sleep sleep sleep sleep sleep

south
남쪽
[sauθ 싸웃쓰]

south   south   south   south

street
거리

[strit 스뜨릿]

street   street   street   street

town
마을

[táun 타운]

town town town town town

vilage
마을, 촌락

[vilidʒ 빌리쥐]

vilage vilage vilage vilage

way
길, 방법

[wei 웨이]

way way way way

welcome
환영하다

[wélkəm 웰컴]

welcome   welcome

west
서쪽

[west 웨스트]

west west west west west

2. 부정문 만드는 법

(a) I am not~ . He is not~

I am not a boy.

I am **a boy.**
[ái æm ə bɔi] 긍정문

나는 소년입니다

I am **not a boy.**
[ái æm nɑːt ə bɔi] 부정문

나는 소년이 아닙니다

I am **a singer.**
[ái æm ə siŋər]

나는 가수입니다

→ I am **not a singer.**
[ái æm nɑːt ə siŋər]

나는 가수가 아닙니다

I am not a singer.

He is not a teacher.

He is **a teacher.**
[hiː iz ə tiːtʃər]

그는 선생님입니다

→ He is **not a teacher.**
[hiː iz nɑːt ə tiːtʃər]

그는 선생님이 아닙니다

I am a boy.   I am a boy.

I am not a boy. I am not a boy.

I am a singer.   I am a singer.

I am not a singer. I am not a singer.

He is a teacher. He is a teacher.

He is not a teacher.

• 부정문 만들기– 'be' 동사가 들어간 문장을 부정문으로 만들 때에는 'be' 동사 바로 뒤에 'not' 만 붙여주면 됩니다. 예를 들어, I am a student. 를 I am not a student. 로 하면 됩니다.

I am not~ . He is not~

She is a nurse. 긍정문
[ʃi iz ə nɜːrs]
그녀는 간호사입니다

→ She is not a nurse. 부정문
[ʃi iz nɑːt ə nɜːrs]
그녀는 간호사가 아닙니다

I am happy.
[ái æm hǽpi]
나는 행복합니다

→ I am not happy.
[ái æm nɑːt hǽpi]
나는 행복하지 않습니다

He is stupid.
[hiː iz stuːpid]
그는 어리석습니다

→ He is not stupid.
[hiː iz nɑːt stuːpid]
그는 어리석지 않습니다

She is a nurse.　She is a nurse.

She is not a nurse. She is not a nurse.

I am happy.　　I am happy.

I am not happy. I am not happy.

He is stupid.　　He is stupid.

He is not stupid.　He is not stupid.

보기와 같이 다음 긍정문을 부정문으로 바꿔 봅시다.

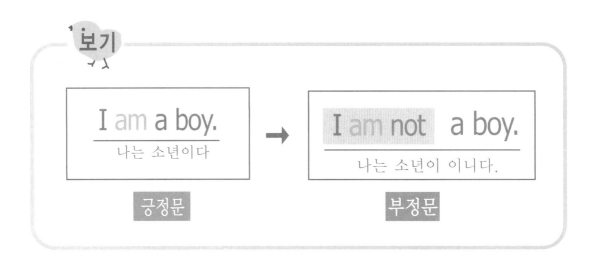

①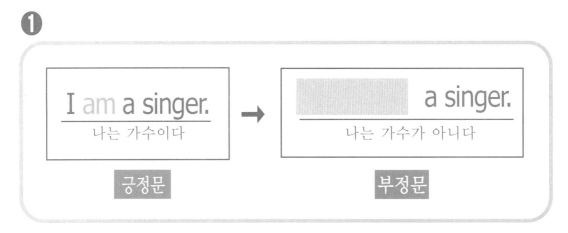

②

❸

She is a nurse.
그녀는 간호사이다

긍정문

→ 　　　　　　 a nurse.
그녀는 간호사가 아니다

부정문

❹

I am happy.
나는 행복하다

긍정문

→ 　　　　　　 happy.
나는 행복하지 않다

부정문

❺

He is stupid.
그는 어리석다

긍정문

→ 　　　　　　 stupid.
그는 어리석지 않다

부정문

대립어1

large
큰

[lɑːrdʒ 라-쥐]

large   large   large   large

small
작은

[smɔːl 스 몰]

small   small   small

thin
얇은

[θin 띤]

thin   thin   thin   thin   thin

thick
두꺼운

[θik 씩]

thick   thick   thick   thick

heavy
무거운
[hévi 헤뷔]

heavy   heavy   heavy

light
가벼운
[lait 라잇트]

light   light   light   light

quick
빠른
[kwik 퀵]

quick   quick   quick   quick

slow
느린
[slou 슬로우]

slow   slow   slow   slow

little
작은
[litl 리를]

little   little   little   little

big
큰, 커다란
[big 빅]

big   big   big   big   big

tall
키가 큰

[tɔːl 톨]

tall tall tall tall

short
짧은, 키가작은

[ʃɔːrt 숄–트]

short short short short

left
왼쪽, 왼쪽의

[left 레프트]

left left left left left left

right
오른쪽

[rait 롸잇트]

right right right right right

down
아래로

[daun 다운]

down down down down

up
위쪽으로

[ʌp 엎]

up up up up up up

under
~의 아래에

[ʌ́ndər 언덜]

under　under　under　under

on
~의 위에

[an 언]

on　on　on　on　on　on

young
젊은, 어린

[jʌŋ 영]

young　young　young　young

old
늙은

[ould 오울드]

old　old　old　old　old　old

true
진실의

[trú: 트루]

true　true　true　true　true

false
거짓의

[fɔ́:ls 폴스]

false　false　false　false

They are children. 긍정문
[ðei ər tʃildrən]
그들은 어린이입니다

They are not children. 부정문
[ðei ər nɑːt tʃildrən]
그들은 아이가 아닙니다

They are brohters.
[ðei ər brʌðərs]
그들은 형제들입니다

They are not brohters.
[ðei ər nɑːt brʌðərs]
그들은 형제가 아닙니다

They are teachers.
[ðei ər tiːtʃərs]
그들은 선생님입니다

They are not teachers.
[ðei ər nɑːt tiːtʃərs]
그들은 선생님이 아닙니다

They are children.   They are children.

They are not children.

They are brohters.   They are brohters.

They are not brohters.

They are teachers.   They are teachers.

They are not teachers.

• be동사는 주어에 따라 달라집니다.

인 칭	뜻	주 격	be동사
1 인 칭	나	I	am
	우리	we	are
2 인 칭	너	you	are
	너희들	you	are

They are not~

They are lazy.
[ðei ər leizi]

그들은 게으릅니다

→ **They are not lazy.**
[ðei ər nɑːt leizi]

그들은 게으르지 않습니다

They are busy.
[ðei ər bizi]

그들은 바쁩니다

→ **They are not busy.**
[ðei ər nɑːt bizi]

그들은 바쁘지 않습니다

They are poor.
[ðei ər pɔːr]

그들은 가난합니다

→ **They are not poor.**
[ðei ər nɑːt pɔːr]

그들은 가난하지 않습니다

문장을 따라 써 보세요

They are lazy.   They are lazy.

They are not lazy. They are not lazy.

They are busy.   They are busy.

They are not busy. They are not busy.

They are poor.   They are poor.

They are not poor. They are not poor.

인 칭	뜻	주 격	be동사
3인 칭	그녀	she	is
	그	he	is
	그것	it	is
	그들	they	are

🐞 보기와 같이 다음 긍정문을 부정문으로 바꿔 봅시다.

보기

They are lazy.	→	They are not lazy.
그들은 게으르다		그들은 게으르지 않다
긍정문		부정문

①

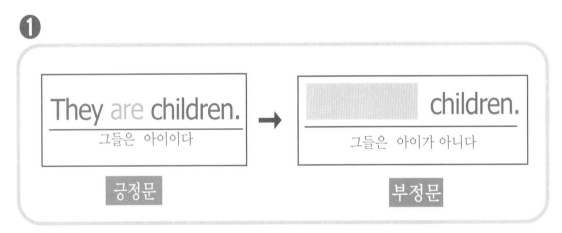

They are children.	→	___ children.
그들은 아이이다		그들은 아이가 아니다
긍정문		부정문

②

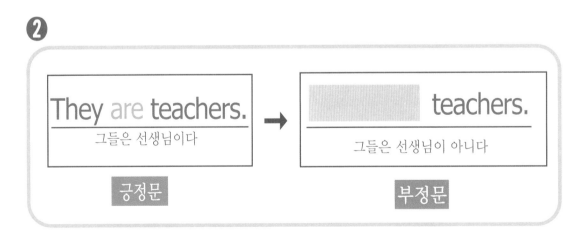

They are teachers.	→	___ teachers.
그들은 선생님이다		그들은 선생님이 아니다
긍정문		부정문

I am not   They are not   She is not

❸

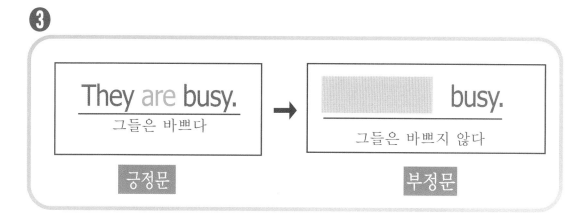

They are busy.
그들은 바쁘다
긍정문

→

_____ busy.
그들은 바쁘지 않다
부정문

❹

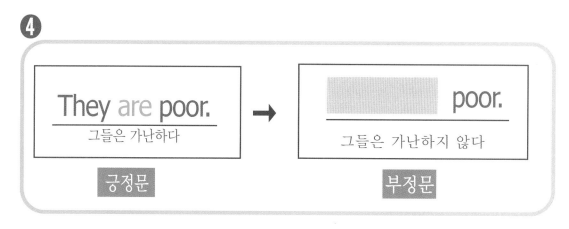

They are poor.
그들은 가난하다
긍정문

→

_____ poor.
그들은 가난하지 않다
부정문

❺

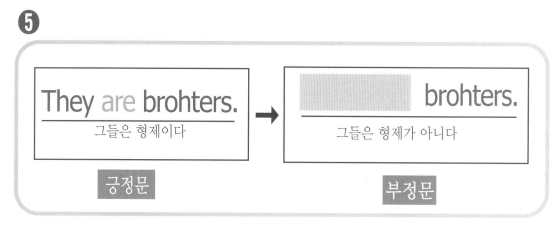

They are brohters.
그들은 형제이다
긍정문

→

_____ brohters.
그들은 형제가 아니다
부정문

단어를 따라 써 보세요

ago
~전에

[əgóu 어고우]

ago   ago   ago   ago   ago

again
다시, 또

[əgén 어게인]

again   again   again   again

also
역시, 또한

[ɔ́ːlsou 오-올쏘우]

also   also   also   also   also

around
~의 주위에

[əráund
어롸운드]

around   around   around

early
이른, 일찍

[ə́ːrli 어얼리]

early   early   early   early

else
그밖에

[els 엘스]

else   else   else   else

ever
이제까지

[évər 에벌]

ever   ever   ever   ever

just
방금, 오직

[dʒʌst 쥐스트]

just   just   just   just

last
마지막으로

[læst 래스트]

last   last   last   last   last

not
아니다, 않다

[nat 낫]

not   not   not   not   not

now
지금, 방금

[nau 나우]

now   now   now   now

off
~떨어져

[ɔːf 어프]

off off off off off off

about
약, 거의

[əbáut 어바웃]

about about about about

across
~의 건너편

[əkrɔ́ːs
어크뤄-스]

across across across across

after
~후에

[ǽftər 애프털]

after after after after after

along
~따라서

[əlɔ́ːŋ 얼러엉]

along along along along

among
~의 사이에

[əmʌ́ŋ 어멍]

among among among among

as
~만큼

[æz 애즈]

as as as as as as as as as

at
~에서

[æt 앳]

at at at at at at at at at

below
~보다 아래에

[bilóu 빌로우]

below below below below

beside
~의 곁에

[bisáid 비싸이드]

beside beside beside beside

by
곁에, ~로써

[bai 바이]

by by by by by by by

for
~을 위해서

[fɔːr 폴]

for for for for for for for

(c) I am not , No, I'm not

Are you a student?
[ər jə ə studnt] 의문문

당신은 학생입니까?

I am not a student.
[ái æm nɑːt ə studnt] 부정문

나는 학생이 아닙니다

No, I'm not.
[nou aim nɑːt] 부정문

아닙니다, 학생이 아닙니다

Are you a student?

Are you a student?

I am not a student.

I am not a student.

No, I'm not.   No, I'm not.

No, I'm not.   No, I'm not.

I am not~ .   He is not~

Are you a nurse?
[ər jə ə nɜs]

당신은 간호사입니까?

I am not a nurse.
[ái æm nɑːt ə nɜs]

나는 간호사가 아닙니다

No, I'm not.
[ər jə ə studnt]

아닙니다, 간호사가 아닙니다

Are you a nurse?

Are you a nurse?

I am not a nurse.   I am not a nurse.

I am not a nurse.   I am not a nurse.

No, I'm not.   No, I'm not.

No, I'm not.   No, I'm not.

보기와 같이 다음 긍정문을 부정문으로 바꿔 봅시다.

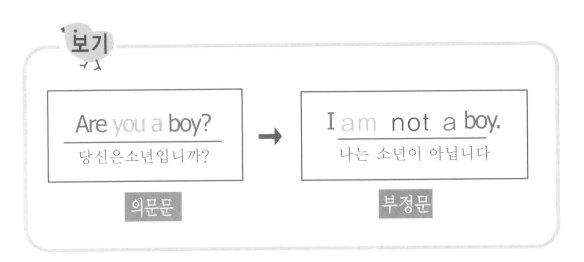

보기

Are you a boy?	→	I am not a boy.
당신은소년입니까?		나는 소년이 아닙니다
의문문		부정문

❶

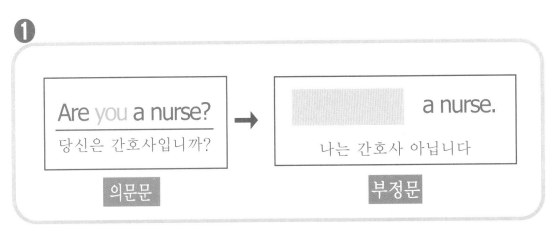

Are you a nurse?	→	▭▭▭ a nurse.
당신은 간호사입니까?		나는 간호사 아닙니다
의문문		부정문

❷

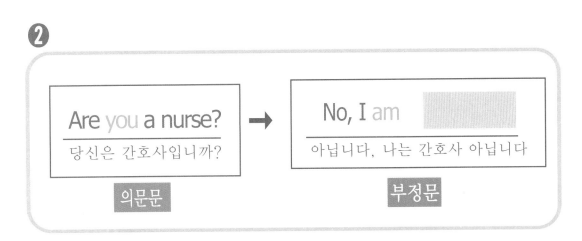

Are you a nurse?	→	No, I am ▭▭
당신은 간호사입니까?		아닙니다, 나는 간호사 아닙니다
의문문		부정문

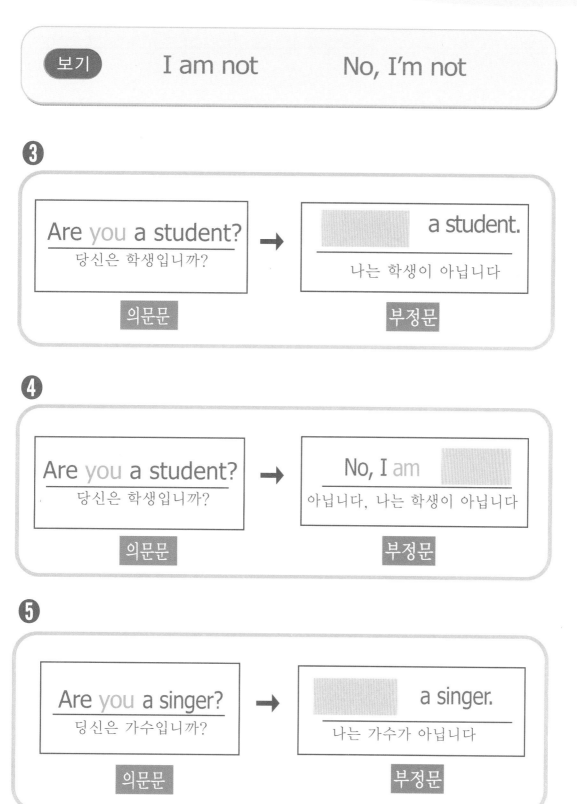

동사 2

act
행동하다
[ækt 액트]

act　act　act　act　act　act

arrive
도착하다
[əráiv 어롸이브]

arrive　arrive　arrive

become
~이 되다
[bikʌ́m 비컴]

become　become　become

bring
가져오다
[briŋ 브링]

bring　bring　bring　bring

broke
깨트렸다
[brouk 브로-크]

broke　broke　broke　broke

close	close close close close close
닫다	
[klouz 클로우즈]	

cross	cross cross cross cross cross
가로지르다	
[crɔːs 크뤄스]	

cut	cut cut cut cut cut cut
베다, 깎다	
[kʌt 컷]	

feel	feel feel feel feel feel
느끼다	
[fiːl 퓌-일]	

fight	fight fight fight fight
싸우다	
[fait 퐈잇트]	

fill	fill fill fill fill fill fill
채우다	
[fil 퓔]	

happen
발생하다
[hǽpən 해쁜]

happen　happen　happen

help
돕다
[help 헬-프]

help　help　help　help　help

hit
때리다
[hit 힛]

hit　hit　hit　hit　hit　hit　hit

knock
두드리다
[nak 낙]

knock　knock　knock　knock

know
알다, 이해하다
[nou 노우]

know　know　know　know

let
시키다
[let 렛]

let　let　let　let　let　let　let

leave
떠나다

[liːv 리-브]

leave leave leave leave leave

like
좋아하다

[laik 라이크]

like like like like like

look
보다

[luk 룩]

look look look look look

make
만들다

[meik 메이크]

make make make make make

move
움직이다

[muːv 무-브]

move move move move move

send
보내다

[send 쎈드]

send send send send send

3. 의문문 만드는 법

(a) Are you ~

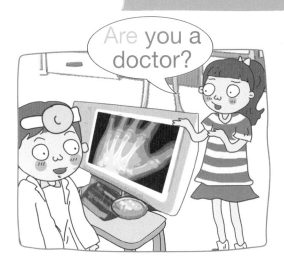

You are a doctor.
[iə ər ə dɑ:ktər]
당신은 의사입니다

→ Are you a doctor?
[ər iə ə dɑ:ktər]
당신은 의사입니까?

He is an actor.
[hi: iz ən: æktər]
그는 배우입니다

→ Is he an actor?
[iz hi: ən: æktər]
그는 배우입니까?

She is a model.
[ʃi iz ə mɑ:dl]
그녀는 모델입니다

→ Is she a model?
[iz ʃi ə mɑ:dl]
그녀는 모델입니까?

You are a doctor. You are a doctor.

Are you a doctor? Are you a doctor?

He is an actor. He is an actor.

Is he an actor? Is he an actor?

She is a model. She is a model.

Is she a model? Is she a model?

Are you ~

You are tired.
[iə ər taiərd]

당신은 피곤합니다

→ **Are you tired?**
[ər iə taiərd]

당신은 피곤합니까?

He is rich.
[hi: iz ritʃ]

그는 부자입니다

→ **Is he rich?**
[iz hi: ritʃ]

그는 부자입니까?

She is sad.
[ʃi iz sæd]

그녀는 슬픕니다

→ **Is she sad?**
[iz ʃi sæd]

그녀는 슬픕니까?

You a re tired.　　You a re tired.

Are you tired?　　Are you tired?

He is rich.　　He is rich.

Ie he rich?　　Ie he rich?

She is sad.　　She is sad.

Is she sad?　　Is she sad?

• 의문문은 묻는 문장입니다. 영어에서 긍정문을 의문문(질문하는 문장)
으로 만들 때에는 '주어'와 '동사'의 순서만 바꾸어 주면 됩니다.
'We are boys.'를 'Are we boys?'와 같이 바꿔줍니다.

보기와 같이 다음 긍정문을 의문문으로 바꿔 봅시다.

보기

He is an actor.
그는 배우입니다
긍정문

→

Is he an actor?
그는 배우인가요?
의문문

❶

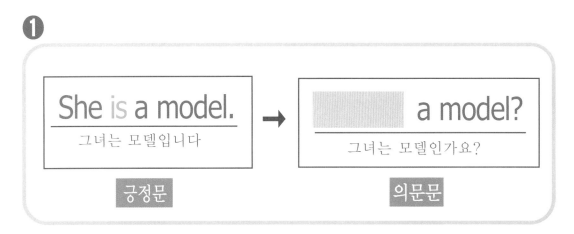

She is a model.
그녀는 모델입니다
긍정문

→

a model?
그녀는 모델인가요?
의문문

❷

She is sad.
그녀는 슬픕니다
긍정문

→

sad?
그녀는 슬픈가요?
의문문

Are you   Is he   Is she

❸

You are a doctor.
당신은 의사입니다

→

☐☐☐☐☐ a doctor?
당신은 의사인가요?

긍정문   의문문

❹

You are tired.
당신은 피곤합니다

→

☐☐☐☐☐ tired?
당신은 피곤한가요?

긍정문   의문문

❺

He is rich.
그는 부자입니다

→

☐☐☐☐☐ rich?
그는 부자인가요?

긍정문   의문문

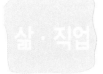

captain
선장, 우두머리

[kǽptin 캡틴]

captain captain captain captain

cook
요리사

[kúk 쿡]

cook   cook   cook   cook

doctor
의사

[dάktər 닥털]

doctor   doctor   doctor

job
일, 직업

[dʒab 좝]

job   job   job   job   job   job

nurse
간호사

[nəːrs 널쓰]

nurse   nurse   nurse   nurse

pilot
조종사

[páilət 파일럿]

pilot   pilot   pilot   pilot   pilot

police
경찰

[pəlíːs 펄리-스]

police   police   police

god
하느님

[gad 가드]

god   god   god   god   god

group
무리, 모임, 떼

[gruːp 구루웁]

group   group   group   group

king
왕

[kiŋ 킹]

king   king   king   king

lead
인도하다

[iːd 리드]

lead   lead   lead   lead   lead

letter
편지
[létər 레럴]

letter   letter   letter   letter

life
생명, 생활
[lɑif 라이프]

life life life life life life life

live
살다
[liv 리브]

live live live live live live

luck
행운
[lɔk 럭]

luck luck luck luck

mail
우편
[meil 메일]

mail mail mail mail mail mail

marry
결혼하다
[mǽri 매뤼]

marry marry marry marry

| **news** 소식 | news news news  |
| [njuːs 뉴-스] | |

| **party** 파티, 모임 | party party party party |
| [páːrti 파-리] | |

| **peace** 평화 | peace peace peace peace |
| [piːs 피-스] | |

| **town** 마을 | town town town town town |
| [táun 타운] | |

| **village** 마을, 촌락 | village village village village |
| [vílidʒ 빌리쥐] | |

| **welcome** 환영하다 | welcome welcome welcome |
| [wélkəm 웰컴] | |

Your sisters are quiet.
[iur ər sistərs ər kwaiət]

당신의 자매들은 조용합니다

Are your sisters quiet?
[ər iur sistərs kwaiət]

당신의 자매들은 조용합니까?

The students are smart.
[ðə stu:dnt∫ ər sma:rt]

그 학생들은 똑똑합니다

Are the students smart?
[ər ðə stu:dnt∫ sma:rt]

그 학생들은 똑똑합니까?

The teachers are kind.
[ðə ti:t∫ərs ər kaind]

그 선생님들은 친절합니까?

Are the teachers kind?
[ər ðə ti:t∫ərs kaind]

그 선생님들은 친절합니까?

Your sisters are quiet.

Are your sisters quiet?

The students are smart.

Are the students smart?

The teachers are kind.

대명사가 어떻게 사용되느냐에 따라 다음과 같이 바뀝니다.

뜻	주격(가,은)	소유격(의)	목적격(을,를)
나	I	my	me
너	you	your	you
그	he	his	him
그녀	she	her	her
그것	it	its	it

Are you ~

The dogs are cute.
[ðər dɔ:gs ər kiu:t]

그 개들은 귀엽습니다

→

Are the dogs cute?
[ər ðər dɔ:gs kiu:t]

그 개들은 귀엽습니까?

The trees are tall.
[ðər tri:s ər tɔ:l]

그 나무들은 큽니다

→

Are the trees tall?
[ər ðər tri:s tɔ:l]

그 나무들은 큽니까?

The rooms are clean.
[ðər ru:ms ər kli:n]

그 방들은 깨끗합니다

→

Are the rooms clean?
[ər ðər ru:ms kli:n]

그 방들은 깨끗합니까?

The dogs are cute.

Are the dogs cute?

The treesare tall. The treesare tall.

Are the trees tall? Are the trees tall?

The rooms are clean.

Are the rooms clean?

뜻	주격(가,은)	소유격(의)	목적격(응,를)
너희	you	your	you
그(녀)들,그것들	they	their	them
우리	we	our	us

보기와 같이 다음 긍정문을 의문문으로 바꿔 봅시다.

보기

Your sisters are quiet. 긍정문

당신의 자매들은 조용합니다

→ Are your sisters quiet? 의문문

당신의 자매들은 조용합니까?

❶

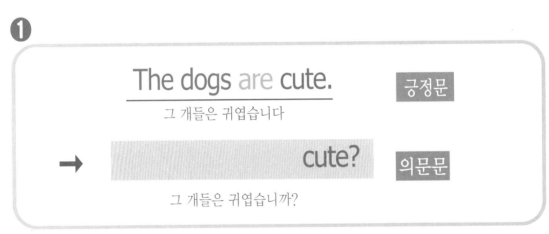

The dogs are cute. 긍정문

그 개들은 귀엽습니다

→ cute? 의문문

그 개들은 귀엽습니까?

❷

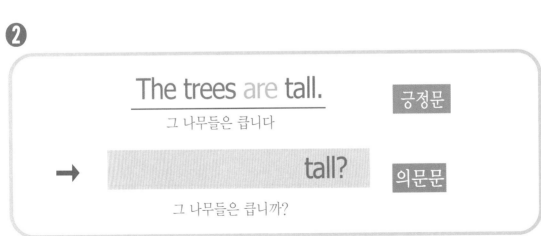

The trees are tall. 긍정문

그 나무들은 큽니다

→ tall? 의문문

그 나무들은 큽니까?

Are the   Is he   Is she

❸

The teachers are kind. 긍정문

그 선생님들은 친절합니다

→ kind? 의문문

그 선생님들은 친절합니까?

❹

The rooms are clean. 긍정문

그 방들은 깨끗합니다

→ clean? 의문문

그 방들은 깨끗합니까?

❺

The students are smart. 긍정문

그 학생들은 똑똑합니다

→ smart? 의문문

그 학생들은 똑똑합니까?

단어를 따라 써 보세요

air
공기

[εər 에얼]

air air air air air

beach
물가, 바닷가

[biːtʃ 비-잇취]

beach beach beach beach

cloud
구름

[klaud 클라우드]

cloud cloud cloud cloud

earth
지구, 땅

[əːrθ 어얼쓰]

earth earth earth

field
들판

[fiːld 필드]

field field field field field

grass
풀
[græs 그뢰쓰]

grass grass grass grass

gold
금
[gould 고울드]

gold gold gold gold

green
녹색
[griːn 그뤼인]

green green green green

hill
언덕
[hil 힐]

hill hill hill hill hill hill

island
섬
[áilənd 아일런드]

island island island island

jungle
밀림, 정글
[dʒʌ́ŋgl 졍글]

jungle jungle jungle jungle

lake
호수

[leik 레익]

lake lake lake lake lake lake

land
땅, 육지

[lænd 랜드]

land land land land

moon
달

[muːn 문]

moon moon moon moon

mountain
산

[mauntən마운튼]

mountain mountain

rainbow
무지개

[réinbóu 뢰인보우]

rainbow rainbow rainbow

river
강

[rívər 뤼벌]

river river river river

sky
하늘

[skai 스까이]

sky sky sky sky sky sky

space
공간, 우주

[speis 스뻬이스]

space space space space

star
별

[sta:r 스딸]

star star star star star

sun
태양, 햇빛

[sʌn 썬]

sun sun sun sun sun sun

water
물

[wɔ́:tər 워-터]

 water water water

world
세계, 지구

[wə:rld 월드]

world world world world

(c) I don't like~

I like pizza.
[ái laik píːtsə]

나는 피자를 좋아합니다

→ Do you like pizza?
[də jə laik píːtsə]

당신은 피자를 좋아합니까?

They like dogs.
[ðei laik dɔːgs]

그들은 강아들을 좋아합니다

→ Do they like dogs?
[də ðei laik dɔːgs]

그들은 개를 좋아합니까?

She likes Spring.
[ʃi laiks spriŋ]

그녀는 봄을 좋아합니다

Does she like Spring?
[dʌz ʃi laik spriŋ]

그녀는 봄을 좋아합니까?

I like pizza.   I like pizza.

Do you like pizza? Do you like pizza?

They like dogs.   They like dogs.

Do They like dogs? Do They like dogs?

She likes Spring. She likes Spring.

Does She likes Spring?

I don't like~

I like reading book.
[ái laik riːdiŋ buk]

나는 책읽기를 좋아합니다

Do you like reading book?
[də jə laik riːdiŋ buk]

당신은 책 읽기를 좋아합니까?

He likes math.
[hiː laiks mæθ]

나는 책읽기를 좋아합니다

Does he like math?
[dʌz hiː laik mæθ]

그는 수학을 좋아합니까?

We like computer.
[wi laiks kəmpjuːtər]

우리는 컴퓨터를 좋아합니다

Do you like computer?
[də jə laiks kəmpjuːtər]

당신들은 컴퓨터를 좋아합니까?

I like reading book.

Do you like reading book?

He likes math.   He likes math.

Does he like math? Does he like math?

We like computer. We like computer.

Do you like computer?

보기와 같이 다음 긍정문을 의문문으로 바꿔 봅시다.

1

2

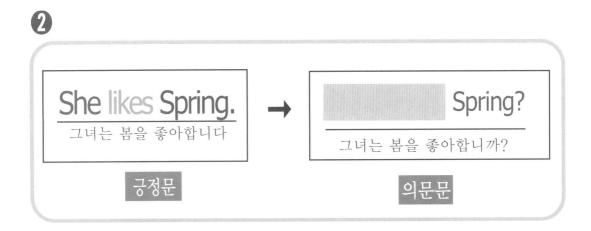

보기

| Do they like | Does she like |
| Do you like | Does he like |

❸

I like reading book.
나는 책 읽기를 좋아합니다

➡

_____ reading book?
당신은 책 읽기를 좋아합니까?

긍정문   의문문

❹

I like computer.
나는 컴퓨터를 좋아합니다

➡

_____ computer?
당신은 컴퓨터를 좋아합니까?

긍정문   의문문

❺

He likes math.
그는 수학을 좋아합니다

➡

_____ math?
그는 수학을 좋아합니까?

긍정문   의문문

단어를 따라 써 보세요

apple
사과

[金pəl] 애쁠

apple apple apple apple apple

butter
버터

[bʌ́tər] 버러

butter　butter　butter　butter

breakfast
아침식사

[brékfəst]
블랙풔스트

breakfast breakfast breakfast

bread
빵

[bred] 브레드

bread　bread　bread

cheese
치즈

[tʃiːz] 취-즈

cheese cheese cheese cheese

cake
케이크

[keik] 케이크

cake cake cake cake

coffee
커피

[kɔ́ːfi] 커-퓌

coffee coffee coffee

cream
크림

[kriːm] 크뤼-임

cream cream cream cream

dinner
저녁 식사

[dínər] 디널

dinner dinner dinner dinner

food
음식

[fuːd] 푸-드

food food food food food

hamburger
햄버거

[hǽmbəːrgər]
햄버거

hamburger hamburger

banana
바나나

[bənǽnə]
버내너

banana　banana

corn
옥수수

[kɔːrn] 콘

corn corn corn corn corn

cocumber
오이

[kjúːkʌmbər]
큐컴벌

cocumber　cocumber

fruit
과일

[fruːt] 푸룻

fruit fruit fruit fruit

grape
포도

[greip] 그뢰입

grape grape grape grape

pear
배

[pɛər] 페얼

pear pear pear pear pear

strawberry
딸기
[strɔ́ːbéri]
스프러-베뤼

strawberry   strawberry

tomato
토마토
[təméitou]
터메이토

tomato   tomato   tomato

lemon
레몬
[lemən]
레먼

lemon lemon lemon lemon

melon
메론
[mélən] 메런

melon melon melon melon

peach
복숭아
[píːtʃ] 피-치

peach peach peach peach

juice
주스
[dʒuːs] 쥬-스

juice juice juice juice

(d) Is it~

Is it a computer?
[iz it ə kəmpiu:tər]
이것은 컴퓨터입니까?

Is it sunny?
[iz it sʌni]
날씨가 맑습니까?

Is it eleven o'clock?
[iz it ilevn əklɑ:k]
11시 정각입니까?

Is it a computer? Is it a computer?

Is it a computer? Is it a computer?

Is it sunny?　　　Is it sunny?

Is it sunny?　　　Is it sunny?

Is it eleven o'clock?

Is it eleven o'clock?

Is it~

Is it heavy?
[iz it hevi]

이것은 무겁습니까?

Yes, it is.
[jes it iz]

예, 그렇습니다

Is it September?
[iz it septembər]

(지금이) 9월입니까?

Yes, it is.
[jes it iz]

예, 그렇습니다

Is it Monday today?
[iz it mʌndi tədei]

오늘은 월요일입니까?

Yes, it is.
[jes it iz]

예, 그렇습니다

Is it heavy?   Is it heavy?

Yes, it is.   Yes, it is.   Yes, it is.

Is it September? Is it September?

Yes, it is.   Yes, it is.   Yes, it is.

Is it Monday today?   Is it Monday today?

Yes, it is.   Yes, it is.   Yes, it is.

🐞 보기에서 골라 　　　　　 속에 알맞은 단어를 쓰고 아래 따라 써 봅시다.

❶ Is it

이것은 컴퓨터입니까?

Is it

❷ Is it

날씨가 맑습니까?

Is it

❸ Is it

이것은 무겁습니까?

Is it

a computer?　　sunny?　　heavy?
it is,　　September?

❹ Yes,

예, 그렇습니다.

Yes,

❺ Is it

지금이 9월입니까?

Is it

❻ Yes,

예, 그렇습니다.

Yes,

단어를 따라 써 보세요

end
끝, 마치다
[end 엔드]

end   end   end   end   end

begin
시작하다
[bigín 비긴]

begin   begin   begin   begin

best
가장 좋은
[best 베스트]

best   best   best   best   best

worst
최악의
[wə́:rst 월스트]

worst   worst   worst   worst

come
오다

[kʌm 컴]

come come come come come

go
가다

[gou 고우]

go go go go go go go

far
멀리

[fɑːr 퐈]

far far far far far far far

near
가까운

[niər 니얼]

near near near near near

poor
가난한

[púər 푸얼]

poor poor poor poor poor poor

rich
돈 많은

[ritʃ 릿취]

rich rich rich rich rich rich

start
출발하다

[staːrt 스딸트]

start start start start start

stop
멈추다

[stap 스땁]

stop stop stop stop

dirty
더러운, 불결한

[dɔ́ːrti 덜티]

dirty dirty dirty dirty dirty

clean
깨끗한

[kliːn 클리인]

clean clean clean clean clean

in
~안에

[in 인]

in in in in in in in in

out
밖으로, 밖에

[aut 아웃]

out out out out out out

push
밀다
[puʃ 푸쉬]

push   push   push   push

pull
당기다
[pul 풀]

pull   pull   pull   pull   pull

sit
앉다
[sit 씻]

sit   sit   sit   sit   sit

stand
서다, 일어서다
[stænd스팬드]

stand   stand   stand   stand

open
열다
[óupən
오우쁜]

open open open open

shut
닫다, 덮다
[ʃʌt 셧]

shut   shut   shut   shut   shut

단어를 따라 써 보세요

captain
선장, 우두머리

[kǽptin 캡틴]

captain   captain   captain

god
하느님

[gad 가드]

god   god   god   god   god

group
무리, 모임, 떼

[gruːp 구루웁]

group   group   group   group

king
왕

[kiŋ 킹]

king   king   king   king   king

news
소식

[njuːz 뉴-즈]

news   news   news

nurse
간호사
[nəːrs 널쓰]

nurse   nurse   nurse

party
파티, 모임
[páːrti 팔티]

party   party   party   party

peace
평화
[piːs 피-스]

peace   peace   peace   peace

town
마을
[táun 타운]

town   town   town   town

village
마을, 촌락
[vílidʒ 빌리쥐]

village   village   village

welcome
환영하다
[wélkəm 웰컴]

welcome   welcome   welcome

자음 발음 기호

[p] 프 [b] 브 [t] 트 [d] 드 [k] 크

[g] 그 [m] 므 [n] 느 [ŋ] 응 [l] 르

[f] 프 [v] 브 [θ] 쓰 [ð] 드 [s] 스

[z] 즈 [ʃ] 쉬 [ʒ] 쥐 [tʃ] 취 [dʒ] 쥐

[r] 르 [h] 흐 [j] 이 [w] 우

모음 발음 기호

[a] 아	[i] 이	[e] 에	[æ] 애	[ɔ] 어/오
[u] 우	[ʌ] 어	[ə] 어	[iː] 이-	[aː] 아-
[ɔː] 오-	[uː] 우-	[au] 아우	[ei] 에이	[ou] 오우
[ai] 아이	[ɔi] 오이	[əːr] 어-ㄹ	[iːr] 이-ㄹ	[iər] 이어ㄹ
[uər] 우어-ㄹ				

자음 발음 기호

[p] 프

pen [pen] [펜] 펜

아랫입술과 윗입술을 붙였다 떼면서 숨을 급히 내쉬듯이 강하게 우리말의 [ㅍ]하고 같은 소리를 내세요.

[b] 브

blue [bluː][블루] 파랑

아랫입술과 윗입술을 붙였다 떼면서 우리 말의 [ㅂ]에 가까운 소리를 내어 보세요.

[d] 드

desk [desk][데스ㅋ]책상

윗니와 아랫니 사이에 혀를 약간 대고 우리 말의 [ㄷ]에 가까운 소리로 발음하세요.

[t] 트

tree[triː] [트리]나무

혀끝을 윗니 뒤에 살짝 붙여서 우리말의 [ㅌ]에 가까운 소리로 발음해 보세요.

[f] 프

fox [faks] [퐈ㄱ쓰]여우

아랫입술을 윗니에 살짝 붙이고 그 사이로 우리말의 [프]와 같이 소리를 내세요.

[k] 크

kid [kid] [키드] 아이

윗니와 아랫니를 약간만 벌리고 혀의 뒷부분을 살짝 들어 우리말의 [ㅋ]과 가까운 소리로 발음하세요.

[l] 르

lemon[lémən][레몬]레몬

아랫입술과 윗입술을 붙였다 떼면서 숨을 급히 내쉬듯이 강하게 우리말의 [ㅍ]하고 같은 소리를 내세요.

[g] 그

grape[greip][그레이프]포도

윗니와 아랫니를 붙이고 혀의 뒷부분을 살짝 들고 우리말의 [ㄱ]과 가까운 소리로 발음하세요.

[ŋ] 응

pink[piŋk][핑크]분홍색

혀의 뒷부분을 입천장 뒤에 살짝 대면서 콧소리로 [응]하고 소리를 내세요.

[m] 므

monkey[mʌŋki][몽키]원숭이

입술을 붙였다 떼면서 콧소리 우리말 [ㅁ]에 가까운 소리를 내세요.

[n] 느

nurse[nəːrs][너얼스]간호사

혀끝을 윗니 뒤에 살짝 대었다 떼면서 콧소리로 우리말의 [ㄴ]에 가까운 소리를 내세요.

[v] 브

vacation [veikéiʃən][붸-케이션]방학

윗니를 아랫입술에 가볍게 대고 우리말의 [ㅂ]에 가까운 소리로 발음해 보세요.

[s] 스

sky[skai][스카이]하늘

윗니와 아랫니를 붙인 사이로 바람을 내보내듯 [스으]하고 소리를 내세요.

[ʒ] 쥐

age[eidʒ][에이쥐]나이

입술을 동그랗게 하고 바람을 내보내듯 [쥐]하고 발음을 해 보세요.

[z] 즈

zebra[ziːbrə][쥐브라]얼룩말

입술을 양옆으로 살짝 당기고, 윗니와 아랫니를 붙인 사이로 바람을 내보내듯 [즈]소리를 내세요.

[θ] 쓰

thin [θin] [씬] 얇은

윗니와 아랫니 사이로 혀끝을 약간 내밀며 [쓰]하고 소리를 내세요.

[ʃ] 쉬

shop [ʃap] [샵] 상점

입술을 동그랗게 하고 바람을 내보내듯 [쉬]하고 발음을 해 보세요.

[ð] 드

that [ðæt] [댓] 저것

윗니와 아랫니 사이로 혀끝을 약간 내밀며 [드]하고 소리를 내세요.

[tʃ] 취

chicken[tʃíkin][취킨]닭

입술을 동그랗게 말아 내밀고
[취]하고 발음해 보세요.

[dʒ] 쥐

juice[dʒuːs][쥬-스]주스

입술을 동그랗게 말아서 숨을
내뱉듯 [쥐]하고 발음해 보세
요.

[r] ㄹ

ruler[rúːlər][룰러]자

혀끝을 살짝 말아 올리면서
우리말의 [ㄹ]을 발음해 보세
요.

[h] ㅎ

hat [hæt] [햇]모자

윗니와 아랫니 사이로 바람을
불어내듯이 [흐]하고 힘있게
발음해 보세요.

[j] 이

yellow[jélou][옐로-우]노랑

우리말 [이]에서 [야]로 자연
스럽게 넘어가듯 발음해 보세
요.

[w] 우

watch[wɑtʃ][왓치]손목시계

입술을 동그랗게 오므리고
[우]하고 소리를 내세요.

모음 발음 기호

[a] 아

shop [ʃɑp] [샵]가게

입을 크게 벌려 입 안쪽에서 [아]하고 소리를 내세요.

[i] 이

ship [ʃip] [쉽] 배

[이]하고 짧게 발음하세요.

[iː] 이-

bee [biː] [비-] 벌

우리 말의 [이]를 길게 끄는 소리와 같이 발음하세요.

[e] 에

egg [eg] [에그]달걀

입을 약간 벌리고 우리 말의 [에]에 가까운 발음으로 소리 내세요.

[æ] 에

apple[æpl][애플]사과

입을 약간 벌리고 우리 말의 [애]와 같은 발음으로 강하게 발음하세요.

[aː] 아-

arm[ɑːrm][아-암]팔

우리 말의 [아]를 길게 끄는 소리와 같이 발음하세요.

[ɔ] 오

soil [sɔil] [소일] 흙

우리 말의 [오]보다 입을 크게 벌리고, 입 안쪽에서 [오]하고 발음해 보세요.

[ɔː] 오-

water [wɔ́təːr] [워럴] 물

입 안쪽에서 [오]하고 길게 발음해 보세요.

[u] 우

cookie [kúki] [쿠키] 쿠키

우리말의 [우]에 가까운 소리이지만 입술을 좀더 좁게 오므리고 발음하세요.

[ʌ] 어

umbrella [mbrélə] [엄브렐러] 우산

우리 말의 [아]와 [어]의 중간 소리로 입을 약간 더 벌리고 [어]에 가깝게 발음하세요.

[ə] 어

lion [láiən] [라이언] 사자

입을 약간 벌리고 혀를 아랫니 뒤에 대고 짧고 약하게 [어]하고 소리를 내세요.

[ai] 아이

kite [kait] [카이트] 연

입을 크게 벌리고 [아]를 강하게 발음하면서 [이]를 약하게 소리 내세요.

[au] 아우

house[haus][하우스]집

[아]를 강하게 발음하고 이어서 [우]를 약하게 소리 내세요.

[ei] 에이

train[trein][트레인]열차

[에]를 강하게 발음하고 이어서 [이]를 약하게 소리 내세요.

[ou] 오우

roa [roud][로드]길

[오]를 강하게 발음하고 이어서 [우]를 약하게 소리 내세요.

[ɔi] 오이

toy [tɔi][토이]장난감

[오]와 [이]를 연이어서 소리를 내세요.

[ɛər] 에어르

airplane[ɛərplèin]
[에어르플레인]비행기

[에]를 강하게 발음하고 이어서 [어ㄹ]를 약하게 소리 내세요.

[uər] 우어르

tour[tuər][투어르] 여행

[우]를 강하게 발음하고 이어서 [어ㄹ]를 약하게 소리 내세요.

[iər] 이어ㄹ

year[jiər][이어ㄹ]해, 1년

[이]를 강하게 발음하고 이어서 [어ㄹ]를 약하게 소리내세요.

[ɔːr] 오어ㄹ

store[stɔr][스토어ㄹ]가게

[오]를 강하게 발음하고 이어서 [어ㄹ]를 약하게 소리내세요.

🎒 해 답

1. 문장의 구조

p. 8p　　We are~ They are~

① We are　　② They are
③ They are　④ We are
⑤ They are　⑥ We are

p. 18p　　play like study

① like　　② play
③ study　④ like
⑤ play　⑥ play
⑦ like

p. 28p　　have has

① have　　② have
③ have　④ have
⑤ have　⑥ have

p. 38p　　Let's Let's go

① Let's go out here.

② Let's go out to play.

③ Let's go camping.

④ Let's study.

⑤ Let's play soccer.

⑥ Let's play baseball.

⑦ Let's eat pizza!

2. 부정문 만드는 법

p. 48p　　a. I am not~ He is not~

① I am not a singer.
② He is not a teacher.
③ She is not a nurse.
④ I am not happy.
⑤ He is not stupid.

p. 58p　　b. They are not~

① They are not children.
② They are not teacher.
③ They are not busy.
④ They are not poor.
⑤ They are not brohters.

p. 68p   I am not ,No,I'm not

① I am not
② No, I'm not
③ I am not
④ No, I'm not
⑤ I am not

3. 의문문 만드는 법

p. 78p   a. Are you ~

① Is she a model?
② Is she sad?
③ Are you a doctor?
④ Are you tired?
⑤ Is he rich?

p. 88p   b. Are you ~

① Are the dogs cute?
② Are the trees tall?
③ Are the teachers kind?
④ Are the rooms clean?
⑤ Are the students smart?

p. 98p   c. I don't like~

① Do they like dogs?
② Does she like Spring?
③ Do you like reading book?
④ Do you like computer?
⑤ Does he like math?

p. 108p   d. Is it~

① a computer?
② sunny?
③ heavy?
④ it is.
⑤ September?
⑥ it is.

초등 영어 문장 규칙 배우기(2)

기초문장 · 단어 따라쓰기

초판 1쇄 발행 2016년 2월 10일

글 Y&M 어학 연구소

펴낸이 서영희 | **펴낸곳** 와이 앤 엠

편집 임명아 | **책임교정** 하연정

본문인쇄 명성 인쇄 | **제책** 정화 제책

제작 이윤식 | **마케팅** 강성태

주소 03659 서울특별시 서대문구 명지2길 21, 102호

전화 (02)308-3891 | Fax (02)308-3892

E-mail yam3891@naver.com

등록 2007년 8월 29일 제312-2007-00004호

ISBN 978-89-93557-69-5   63740